Love Your Sensitivity: 7 Essential Life Changes to Make after Learning You're a Highly Sensitive Person

Arcadia Page

Published by Arcadia Page, 2022.

LOVE YOUR SENSITIVITY: 7 ESSENTIAL LIFE CHANGES TO MAKE AFTER LEARNING YOU'RE A HIGHLY SENSITIVE PERSON

First edition. October 22, 2022.

ISBN: 979-8215260982

Written by Arcadia Page.

Also by Arcadia Page

Idealist Dreams: How I Learned to Plan as an INFP
I Want to Do All the Things: Finding Balance as a Polymath,
Multipotentialite & Renaissance Soul
I Can't Help Being an INFP Writer
The Little Book of Tiny Tasks: Make Your Life More Calm While
Getting Things Done 5 Minutes at a Time
Thoughtful Planning: How to Use Questions for Self-reflection to
Design Your Day
Love Your Sensitivity: 7 Essential Life Changes to Make after Learning
You're a Highly Sensitive Person

Watch for more at www.arcadiapage.com.

Table of Contents

This book is dedicated to my dear husband, who is always reminding me that I'm inherently worthy of love.

Introduction

When I discovered I was a highly sensitive person, I thought I had myself *all* figured out. I was eager to do everything to support my sensitive nature. I added more outdoor time to my life. I installed blue light filters on my devices since I know how visually sensitive I am. I switched to using more natural skin care products since I find too many unnatural chemicals and scents irritating.

These changes were good for me, and I took these steps with the idea that this was the best way to cater to my needs as an HSP. Most of the books I've read about sensitivity focus on creating a comfortable physical environment. HSPs need physical comfort. I'm not downplaying that at all.

But over time, I realized that these surface-level changes don't address the nature of being highly sensitive. Making these kinds of adjustments without paying attention to the underlying facets of sensitivity left me open to hurting myself. I fell into overwork and ignored my needs without realizing it because I thought I was doing what I needed to take care of myself as a sensitive person. As long as I was using all-natural organic soap and toothpaste, everything was good.

Making these shallow gestures toward my sensitivity distracted me from the deep-reaching impacts of being highly sensitive. I didn't fully understand how much my sensitivity interacted with every part of my life.

This book is like a kind letter to a fellow sensitive friend. I want to share all I wish I had done after learning about my sensitivity so others won't experience as much pain from ignorance as I have. And once that ignorance is gone, it's easier to see what a beautiful gift being a highly sensitive person can be.

Like all books of this type, some things from my experience will resonate with you and some won't. That's okay. Take what fits your life and leave the rest. And of course, nothing in this book is to be taken as medical advice. What I'm sharing here is my own experience and thoughts. Your medical decisions are 100% your choice and your responsibility, as they should be.

So here are some lessons learned.

Life Change #1: Know the Signs of Mistaking Your Sensitivity

If you're highly sensitive, here are some traits to look out for that show you may not fully understand your sensitivity. All of these don't have to be present at the same time. Just one may be a signal that you need to step back and re-evaluate how you're handling your sensitivity:

- You feel like you are striving all the time. You're always pushing yourself to wake up, do tasks, or be there for others.
- You are constantly forcing yourself to stay awake. You may even use digital devices when tired to keep your eyes open.
- You are consuming a lot of sugar or caffeine to keep going or just because you feel like it. You may crave these things when tired.
- Your brain feels like an overflowing bathtub.
- You have a lot of neck, shoulder, back, and jaw tension.
- You feel irritable or angry, and you don't know why.
- You are concerned with perfectionism and getting things just right to the point that it's causing you constant anxiety.
- Things not going according to plan feels unbearable.
- You feel creatively dull or uninspired.
- At the edge of your mind is a sense of panic. Panic that everything may go wrong, and you don't have the resources to handle it.
- The emotional energy of others hits you hard. You easily take on the pain and anxiety of others. The emotional walls between you and others feel thin.

Looking at this list, it becomes clear why HSPs often decide to work for themselves. As an HSP, it's essential to structure your life so that you can work at your own speed instead of having others dictate that pace for you. I learned the hard way that if I don't honor my natural pacing, my body will force me to.

Reacquainting myself with my sensitive nature has been both difficult and exhilarating. Accepting my natural pace has been a struggle, but at the same time, I feel so much better when I go with it. Next are the things I wish I would have done to better honor my sensitivity from the start (besides adding blue light filters to all my devices).

As an HSP, it's essential to structure your life so you can work at your own pace.

Life Change #2: See If You're High Sensation Seeking

I f you are an HSS HSP, like I am, you have to approach being sensitive differently from someone who is not. For one thing, **under-stimulation** can end up being as much of a problem as **overstimulation.** As a high sensation seeker, I have to watch out for instigating my overstimulation, especially when facing boredom. I like action, movement, and noise. However, I have to be aware of my thresholds. Sometimes when I listen to music, I start playing it loud, but as time goes on, I have to lower the volume and lower it some more, and then I reach a point where listening to it is irritating. I often jump into things with full intensity but then have to slow my pace or "lower the volume."

If you're an HSS HSP, pay attention to how you deal with quiet and boredom. Find ways to deal with under-stimulation without pushing yourself into overstimulation. You can take this test[1] to see if you are high sensation seeking at Dr. Elaine Aron's website, who is also the author of **The Highly Sensitive Person.**

Another thing to remember about being high sensation seeking is that modern society is built to exploit it. Noise, speed, and flashiness are highly valued, and as an HSS HSP, some of these things are attractive. But get too close for too long, and you will get burned. Your high sensation-seeking tendencies do not cancel out your sensitivity. You're still a highly sensitive person, and that has to be respected.

The biggest challenge has been creating space for my sensation-seeking and sensitivity to work together. Despite the desire for action, when

---

1. https://hsperson.com/test/high-sensation-seeking-test/

you're an HSS HSP, having plenty of mental space is crucial because you need it to check in with yourself and accommodate both tendencies.

You have to be able to tell when it's appropriate to go hard and loud or embrace slowness and quiet. It's a dance that can take some work. However, I do my best when I give my sensitivity the honor it deserves. My high sensation seeking and sensitivity are a team brought together with love.

When my high sensation seeking self notices that my sensitive self is worn out, instead of pushing for more or saying, "What's wrong with you? You can handle it!" it does the loving thing. It says, "I see you're tired, overwhelmed, and frazzled. I'll back off for now. Let's take a break so you can stay healthy."

Neither side can be dominating or inflexible. Both have to work together and acknowledge the needs of the other. There's a reason why I include forceful pushing through life as one of my warning signs. This is a signal that you are either ignoring or bullying your sensitive side, regardless of if you're high sensation seeking or not.

Here are the three pieces of advice that have helped me the most with balancing my high sensation seeking with my sensitivity:

I may love to move fast, but if I slow down my mind and body, I will find balance.

As an HSS HSP, it's easy to feel like a teetering, frazzled weirdo, but taking time throughout the day to slow down and reflect can stop the roller coaster in a good way. And slowing down doesn't have to be boring. I often find sitting out in nature, going for a walk, or hanging out in bed with a good story, relaxing enough to slow me down, but stimulating enough to keep me from being bored.

8

And the best thing about these activities is that they give me time to check in with myself and see what I really need. I may think I'm tired, but after taking a moment to slow down, I find myself with an unexpected burst of energy. On the other hand, after slowing down, I may see that I need a nap. Doing this keeps me in touch with the needs of both my sensitivity and high sensation seeking.

Let go. It's okay that I can't control it all. The world will keep spinning, and I'm where I need to be right now.

In this book, I've written a whole chapter about the importance of learning to let go as an HSP. However, this specific advice has helped me as an HSS HSP because when I'm feeling stretched to my limit, it's because I'm running everywhere, trying to control everything. This reminds me that running is unnecessary. It's okay to take it slow, and things will end up where they need to be if I listen to my natural pace.

And the strange thing is that when I slow down, I often do exactly what I need to do. It may not be what I *want* to do, but it will always be what I need at that moment.

Interruption can be divine.

Since I'm high sensation seeking, I feel like I am full of internal interruptions. I can be focused on enjoying something, but suddenly I feel hungry or tired. Pretty normal stuff. But instead of kindly taking care of myself, I feel irritated that I'm being interrupted by my needs.

This can go the other way around too. For a while, I tried having regular daily rest times, but I couldn't make it work. Whenever I was attempting to rest, I would come up with the most fascinating ideas, or I would feel like going outside or doing anything else that didn't involve just laying there.

However, I've learned to appreciate that these "interruptions" are signals of what I need at the moment. They are invitations to stop and express care. Being interrupted with hunger, tiredness, ideas, and friends are sometimes opportunities to show a little love towards parts of our lives that are essential in their own right.

Of course, not all interruptions are good, but it's helpful to take a closer look at the things that are commonly viewed as interruptions. Are they really taking you away from something important? Or are they creating brief windows to step away and take care of something more—human?

So these are the three concepts that have helped me the most. I keep them written down for easy reference when I feel overwhelmed from trying to please my sensitivity and sensation seeking.

High sensation seeking and sensitivity are a team brought together with love.

Life Change #3: Take an Honest Look at Your Diet

What do you eat when you're feeling tired or anxious? Do you reach for something sweet or caffeinated? Over the past couple of years, I realized that this was me. When feeling overstimulated, I would go for the sugar. Chocolate was my especially favorite weapon of choice. 80% Cacao? YES.

However, using food to deal with overstimulation can backfire. My eating habits only served to numb me. I was avoiding the real issues, which were my need for rest and quiet.

Not resting enough came back to bite me, manifesting as severe muscle aches, anxiety, and a host of other physical problems. As an HSP, it's essential to stay in touch with your sensitivity. Sensitivity is key to staying healthy and is an intricate part of who you are. Although it's painful sometimes, it's better to face it instead of numbing yourself.

If you're an HSS HSP, also try to notice if you're turning to sugar and caffeine not only from tiredness but also to remedy boredom from under-stimulation.

Cut back on (or eliminate) the caffeine. I'm serious.

When I was still a caffeine consumer, I used to scoff at reducing my caffeine intake, although it's commonly recommended for HSPs not to consume it.

I believed that having caffeine was okay for me. I wasn't taking in enough for it to make me feel overwhelmed. I could handle it. However, I didn't understand that I was consuming caffeine to dull my sensitivity.

As a result, I ended up becoming badly addicted to caffeine. A hypoglycemic episode forced me off of it, and the withdrawal process was painful.

So if you are an HSP and think you can handle consuming caffeine, I recommend checking in with yourself. Are you using caffeine to keep your sensitivity at bay and to hide how much rest you need? If so, you'll be much better off reducing or eliminating the caffeine and honestly working with your needs as a sensitive person instead of trying to suppress them.

Because of my circumstances, I came off caffeine almost cold turkey. I don't recommend this. I did it because I had to. I wish I could have had a gradual reduction instead. When the withdrawals were intense, sometimes I would have a cup of green tea. Then I slowly phased out the green tea until I was free. You can find many methods of reducing caffeine intake by doing research online.

In my new caffeine-free life, I currently enjoy drinking Teeccino mixed with a little bit of cold brewed Swiss processed decaf coffee. And as for dark chocolate, I rarely eat it.

So don't use caffeine as a crutch and work with who you are. If your dependence on caffeine comes from the pressure to feel productive, skip ahead and read the chapters *Reevaluate Your Attitude Towards Rest* and *You are Productive*.

Ways to Wake Up in the Morning Without Caffeine

- Take a shower

- Do dry brushing and then take a shower

- Drink a full glass of water after waking up

- Use energizing body or facial wash

- Do aromatherapy with citrus scents

- Take some time to sit outside in the sun

- Generously show some love towards those you live with.

- Listen to your favorite music or read a few pages of a favorite book

- Eat some of your favorite breakfast foods

- Stretch or exercise

Honestly work with your needs as a sensitive person instead of trying to suppress them

Life Change #4: Know How You are the Most Sensitive

When I started learning about my sensitivity, I thought I needed to do what it seemed like all the other HSPs were doing. I believed I needed noise-canceling earphones and other methods of sensory deprivation. I've learned that although I am sensitive to noise and visual stimulation, I don't have to obsess over blocking everything out when I'm overstimulated.

As an HSS HSP, I need awareness of both under-stimulation and overstimulation. Bass-heavy pop music can get tiring for me, although I love it. Yet, I can listen to piano sounds, lo-fi hip-hop, and natural noises all day. Scrolling through social media may give me visual overload, but admiring artwork in a graphic novel or creating art of my own does not.

Also, it's important to note that not all HSPs are sensitive in the same ways. My areas of the most sensitivity are visual and auditory, so when I feel overwhelmed, paying attention to these areas works best for me. But others may be more sensitive to scents, textures, or tastes.

Knowing the physical senses that impact me the most has made me aware of the best ways to soothe myself. Our physical senses aren't all or nothing. They run on a spectrum. The important thing to know is where on that spectrum you feel comfortable and where you feel pushed into overstimulation.

Some Thoughts on Being Sensitive to Chemicals and Substances

I've found that when it comes to medication and herbs, I often need lower doses than average. When I have a headache, a half dose of painkillers does the job. Even when I'm just making a relaxing cup of herbal tea, I brew it at half the strength, especially if I want to be relaxed and not knocked out for the rest of the day.

Years ago, I noticed that the strong fragrances used in shampoo and conditioners aggravated my allergies, so I had to switch to more natural products. So pay close attention to how you react to any herbs and medicines you take and the products you use. As an HSP, your body is more reactive than most people's, so pay attention to what's going on with your body instead of dismissing it.

Pay attention to what's going on with your body instead of dismissing it

Life Change #5: Revaluate Your Attitude Towards Rest

Modern society has issues with rest. Often rest is confused with laziness, procrastination, and addiction to convenience. However, for HSPs, rest is vital. HSPs need rest to keep overstimulation in check and to maintain their focus.

So pay attention to your attitude towards rest. Are popular views of rest affecting how you take care of yourself? Are you pushing yourself to keep going, even when you know you shouldn't? When you take a moment to rest, do you feel guilt nagging in the back of your mind? Do you reluctantly go to bed? Do you resist stopping to recharge?

If so, you may need to readjust your feelings towards resting. Instead of thinking about what you're missing out on or illusions of falling behind, think of how taking a moment to recharge will make you powerful.

Also, don't forget to get in touch with your emotions. This counts as rest as well. Rest time doesn't have to take long. Even closing your eyes for five minutes is enough to make a difference.

Making Naps Awesome

I have a strong natural drive to keep going even when I'm exhausted. In the past, I believed that taking naps was a boring waste of time. I mean, what's fun about sleeping?

But as I faced the reality of my sensitivity, I realized that this mindset had to change. Taking naps when tired is one of the best energy boosts out there. Learning to take brief and effective power naps is important for highly sensitive people because it rejuvenates your body, allows you to release stress, and is an opportunity to get a break from all of the stimulation you've been encountering during the day.

Building appreciation for naps has not been easy for me, but here are things that have helped me to have a better attitude toward it.

Changing the mindset.

Coming from a busy western society, it's easy to look at naps as unproductive. However, to be a healthy HSP, it's necessary to challenge that line of thinking.

Here are some thoughts I like to keep in mind when I'm taking a nap to help me have a better attitude:

- It's okay for me to feel tired. The more tired I am, the better my nap will be.

- I love how I can think more clearly and get more done after having some sleep.

- The world is full of so much busyness. Taking a break from it all is a smart move.

- I am physically preparing for what's coming next in my day.

- Knowing when my body and mind need rest and having the courage to honor that shows that I'm strong, not weak.

- Taking a nap gives me space to temporarily surrender to whatever is here.

Are any other motivational benefits of napping coming to your mind? If so, write them down. Then you can read them over whenever you find yourself resisting taking a snooze.

Aim to Be a Master at Napping

Working to be good at something always motivates me to do my best, even if it's something as simple as napping. But sometimes, napping isn't all that simple. Here are some basic techniques to keep in mind to ensure that your nap leaves you restored and not drained.

- If at all possible, don't nap for more than 30 minutes. If you sleep longer, you're more likely to feel groggy when you wake up and can throw off your nocturnal sleep schedule. **Always set a timer when you nap to avoid oversleeping.**

- Try your best not to nap after 3 pm. Napping later than this can disturb your sleep.

- Have a basic sleep kit. An eye-mask and earplugs are great for having a quality nap. If you find yourself falling asleep in your car or at a desk, carry your sleep kit with you in your bag. If you can take naps in bed, but don't want to be disturbed by daily noises in your house or neighborhood, buy earplugs that will accommodate side sleeping and the other positions you take as you sleep.

- Give yourself a little time to fully wake up after your nap. Don't jump full tilt back into your day. Slowly ease into it.

Have an Amazing Sleep Kit

Under the last point, I mentioned that all you really need for an effective sleep kit is an eye-mask and some earplugs. But here are some other things you can add to your sleep tool repertoire:

- Listen to a sleep podcast. My favorite podcast is the Deep Sleep Sounds podcast. And just so you know, there are eye-masks with Bluetooth earphones built into them, so you can comfortably sleep with the sound surrounding you. If you're sleeping lying down, **avoid using earphones with cords** because that can be a choking hazard.

- If you tend to take naps sitting up, get a travel neck pillow to avoid getting a cramp in your neck.

- Use your nap as a chance to use a facial mask. I particularly like using puffiness-reducing eye-masks. There's nothing like waking up after a nap and having fresh, clear skin around your eyes.

- If you can nap lying down, another fun thing to experiment with is using an acupressure mat.

If you take a moment for a nap, but find that you are struggling to drift off, don't stress about it. It's okay if you don't fall asleep. Simply the act of resting is enough. At the start, I used to struggle to fall asleep, but now it comes more easily to me. So be patient with yourself.

Listening to a sleep podcast is good for keeping whirling thoughts at bay when trying to nap. Another technique I like is if my mind is chattering endlessly after trying to nap for 15 minutes, I'll get up and do a short brain dump in my journal. After that, I set a timer for 15 minutes and try napping again. Usually, I fall asleep after doing the brain dump.

I've written quite a few articles on the importance of rest. Although these posts were created for those with the INFP personality type, these tips can be helpful to anyone. Here they are if you would like to check them out:

- Why Breaks are Essential for Me as an INFP[1]

1. https://arcadiapage.com/2020-12-29-how-to-use-breaks-to-reduce-infp-stress/

- How to Deal With INFP Burnout at Work[2]

- What INFPs Can Do When Feeling Burned Out From Thoughts and Emotions[3]

- How I Plan to Slow Down Today[4]

2. https://arcadiapage.com/2021-07-29-how-to-deal-with-infp-burnout-at-work/

3. https://arcadiapage.com/2022-04-30-what-infps-can-do-when-feeling-burned-out-from-thoughts-and-emotions/

4. https://arcadiapage.com/2018/09/how-i-plan-to-slow-down-today.html

Taking a moment to recharge will make you powerful

Life Change #6: Find a Bodyworker ASAP

I used to think that getting a massage was only for people with extra income who didn't know what to do with their time. But, after getting my first massage, all I could say was, "Why didn't I do this *earlier*?"

HSPs carry a lot of stress in their bodies because they're always trying to steel themselves in a world that is too loud, fast, and busy. In stressful situations, we tend to clench our muscles. HSPs experience more stress due to the mental load of processing so much.

Getting a massage will remove that stress from your body pronto. This is important because it's hard to do this on your own. Acupuncture also works very well.

If you can't afford a massage therapist or an acupuncturist, see if there is a massage therapy or acupuncturist school in your area. I regularly get acupuncture from students under the supervision of licensed acupuncturists, and they do a great job. Rates for bodyworkers in training are much less, plus you're helping someone else to continue their education.

When you get treatment from a bodyworker, don't do so passively. Ask questions about what you can do to relieve muscle tension in between treatments. Pay attention to how the bodyworker takes care of you, note what products they use, and see if you can bring some of their techniques home with you.

I like viewing every acupuncture session as an educational moment. I've learned which Chinese oils relax my muscles the best and how paying attention to parts of my body that seem totally unrelated to my pain can make a huge difference. For one thing, I had no idea that my ongoing neck tension was caused by trigger points in my hands and arms. Not only did that piece of knowledge blow me away, but it also made me way more skilled at taking care of myself. I know what points I need to massage in between visits, and doing so has helped me heal even when I'm not in the office.

In general, be aware of the need to relieve physical tension from your body every day. Taking relaxing baths instead of showering can help, and so can doing stretches. But having a professional on your side will help you take care of yourself on a deeper level.

Questions about Acupuncture and Massage Answered

Does getting acupuncture hurt?

In general, no, it doesn't. Sometimes when a needle is inserted, you may feel a prick or a zing, depending on how tense the area is, but any pain should be minimal. Acupuncturists are trained to do whatever they can to make you feel comfortable. If any of the needles hurt, let them know, and they'll adjust or remove it.

Do I have to take off my clothes?

Depends. For massages, generally yes. For most acupuncture treatments, I've had to remove my clothes, but once in a while, I don't have to.

What do I need to do before an appointment?

Before an acupuncture appointment, avoid exercising heavily, eating a big meal, and drinking anything with caffeine or alcohol. If you want more details on what to do before coming in, ask your acupuncturist or massage therapist.

What do I need to do after an appointment?

You may feel sore after getting a massage. Drinking plenty of water and taking a warm bath or shower can help.

Acupuncture affects people differently. Some report feeling sluggish, others report feeling energized, and others say they feel no change.

I definitely fall into the sluggish category. After getting acupuncture, I take a nap. It's generally recommended not to do heavy exercise and eat a heavy meal after acupuncture. Also, like when getting a massage, drink plenty of water after treatment.

There have been times after getting acupuncture when I've felt ravenously hungry. In that case, I snack here and there until I feel satisfied, being careful not to overeat.

Of course, also ask your bodyworker what to expect after being treated.

How long does it take to know if seeing a bodyworker is making a difference in my health?

This probably varies by person, but for me, three to six visits are enough to know if it's working. One visit is not enough. It takes multiple visits to a bodyworker to see a difference.

How do I find an acupuncturist or a massage therapist?

You can ask your friends if they have any recommendations. I've had a lot of success looking for professionals with good reviews on Google. When I read the reviews, I try to notice if the people who left comments have issues similar to mine.

I also check how I feel as I read a listing and look at the photos. Is this a place I feel attracted to, or is there something about it that makes me uneasy?

Following reviews and checking how I feel has helped me find excellent bodyworkers who are just right for me.

Be aware of the need
to relieve physical
tension from your body
every day

Why Sensitive People are Attracted to Holistic Health Systems

Sensitive people are keenly aware of the interconnected nature of their bodies.

My emotions are not only in my head. They make my muscles tense or relax. They can cause my stomach to feel uncomfortable or my heart to race. They make my breathing deep and calm or rapid and shallow.

Food is not only about my digestive system. The wrong foods can cause my skin to break out with eczema or make me feel anxious or fatigued. Nothing is boxed away on its own. Obviously, this is true for all humans, but I think because of our natural sensitivity, HSPs notice it more.

The wrong skin care products or clothing textures can cause irritability. Grating noises and intense visuals and scents can cause discomfort and headaches. And the negative emotions that arise from sensory irritation can cause more physical problems, creating an ugly feedback cycle.

I find holistic approaches attractive because I know my emotions affect my body and my body influences my feelings, so I need ways to regulate the two in concert. Having suffered from chronic pain, I know how physical pain can make me grouchy and how the stress from that only makes my body hurt more due to muscle tension. I cannot separate one from the other.

My favorite holistic health approaches are Traditional Chinese Medicine and Ayurveda. I like these systems and how they have improved my relationship with my sensitivity. Here is a short introduction to both of them.

Traditional Chinese Medicine

I was introduced to TCM through acupuncture. What I like about TCM is how it considers your diet, mental health, sleep hygiene, and natural constitution.

For example, thanks to my acupuncture visits, I learned that although I tend to feel physically cold because of my high energy levels, I sometimes have too much *fire*.

I was amazed at how well this observation associated my body with my HSS HSP tendencies. Being an HSP is my sensitivity to cold. Being high sensation seeking is my energetic fire.

So my treatment for chronic pain went from regularly using a heating pad on my achy muscles to using White Flower Oil, a topical analgesic with a strong cooling sensation. The difference was noticeable immediately. After having treatment tailored to my nature, I slowly began to heal. I also love how in TCM there is a lot of focus on the healing powers of rest and relaxation, something modern life often undervalues.

When I arrive at the acupuncturist feeling stressed and tired, they work on stimulating acupressure points that relax me. If I'm not sleeping, they also prescribe Chinese herbs that will help. Even during the actual treatment, I'm asked, "Are you comfortable? Are you relaxed?"

It took me a long time to see the connection between comfort, relaxation, and good health. Not long after I started being treated with TCM, I was introduced to this Chinese proverb:

Tension is who you think you should be. Relaxation is who you are.

This is a saying all highly sensitive people need to take to heart.

TCM is complex, so get treatment from a professional. Do not randomly buy Chinese medicinal herbs for yourself. It's better to have them prescribed by a licensed practitioner.

If you would like to learn more about the basics of TCM, I recommend reading **The Ancient Healing Companion** by Misha Ruth Cohen. This book is simple and authoritative. It also shares ways to bring TCM into your daily life.

In the chapter on my favorite self-care practices, I share some TCM-inspired activities that I like to do.

Ayurveda

Ayurveda is a traditional medical system from India. Like TCM, Ayurveda also puts a lot of emphasis on your natural constitution, diet, and sleep habits. In Ayurveda, your constitution is called a *dosha*. There are three doshas: Vata, Pitta, and Kapha. You can have one dominant dosha, or you can also have a blend of two or all three doshas. Your dominant dosha can also shift according to the weather and the seasons.

I originally discovered Ayurveda when I was doing some research on how to improve my diet. I had purchased a few books on Ayurveda, but I found the diet and lifestyle recommendations too varied and complex for my daily life. I was off and on with it for a while and didn't see noticeable improvements.

However, two things happened that changed my experience with Ayurveda. First, through TCM, it became clear that I have more than one dosha. I thought I was Vata only, but I discovered that I am the Pitta dosha too.

The second thing is that around the same time, I came across the book **Ayurveda Everyday** by Monica Bloom.

I like this book because it's simple, to the point, and tailored to modern life. The tips in this book focus on the best practices for each dosha. As a result, I noticed a difference when applying the lifestyle advice. It also helped me to begin reconciling the conflict between my needs as a highly sensitive person and as a high sensation seeker.

I've learned not to get hung up on what is my most dominant dosha. There are plenty of online tests you can take to see which dosha is prominent. However, it's easy to make the mistake of focusing so much on the main dosha that you ignore balancing the other two.

What helped was paying more attention to which dosha feels the most like me each day. Before eating breakfast, I would note which dosha I felt was the most prominent and then adjust my breakfast accordingly. Then around lunch, I would check in again to see which dosha was the most noticeable and use that to determine what I needed to do to bring myself back into balance.

This is also a great way to approach things if you are a blend of doshas and are unsure of which is the most like you. By doing this, I could see that I'm usually either Vata or Pitta. When I feel too much Vata, I slow down and get cozy with something warm and comforting. When I feel too much Pitta, I need to cool down and stop trying to control everything.

And to be clear, when I use the word balance, I don't mean facing everything in a stoic, emotional-less way. I don't mean feeling calm all the time or giving equal energy to everything either. To me, balance is the ability to regain equilibrium. Ayurveda has helped me improve at riding the waves of my emotions and getting back up when I'm knocked over by them.

Ayurveda is easier to practice at home than TCM. I also appreciate its focus on eating the right foods and building healthy daily routines. And you don't have to do everything perfectly to improve your life. A few changes can make a positive impact.

Overall, the mind/body/emotions approach gives clear and systematic ways of handling the intricacies of being an HSP.

Tension is who you think you should be. Relaxation is who you are.

Some of My Favorite Self-Care Practices

For highly sensitive people, self-care is much more than a nice thing to do on the weekend to relax. For me, self-care is self-healing. It's all the things I need to do to heal myself from mental, emotional, and physical stress.

Look at self-care as a regular opportunity to release tension in your body and improve your health. I don't do all of these daily, but I try to do at least one of these activities every day.

Reflection time

This is probably the simplest self-care activity on this list. Take a break from your phone, computer, planner, entertainment, and other things, and spend time with your personal thoughts.

Since I'm high-sensation seeking, I sometimes don't enjoy only sitting there. However, I love pairing my reflection time with a cup of tea, wandering around outside, or enjoying the feeling of sunshine on my body.

At first, my mind is focused on what I'm seeing, drinking, or feeling, but as time goes on my mind starts to wander, and I simply let it do that.

After spending so much time taking in information online, reading, and trying to get things done, it's nice giving my brain some space to do whatever for a while. Sometimes I think about specific things, but often I have no agenda.

My reflection time typically lasts from five to ten minutes. Some days I only do it once. On other days, I do it multiple times. It all depends on what I feel I need.

Going for a walk

Walking is great because it is a good companion activity for reflection time and the easiest form of exercise to access. If I can't do more formal workouts, I sometimes walk to make up for it.

I like walking outdoors the most because of the fresh air, sunshine, and greenery. But when the weather isn't cooperating, I'll hop on my walking exercise machine. It's not the same, but it's better than nothing.

If I'm not using walking as an opportunity to reflect on my day, I'll take that time to listen to an audiobook or podcast.

Gua Sha

After a day of looking at screens and dealing with noise, taking a moment to do a Gua Sha facial massage is relaxing. Doing so helps to release the tension we tend to hold in our faces. This is especially good after a day of talking, smiling, and needing to be socially on.

To do Gua Sha, you will need the following:

- A GuaSha massage tool. Buy a tool that is made of genuine jade or another stone. GingerChi is the brand of GuaSha massage tools I like to use. I especially like how their tools come with a clear instruction page.
- A natural face oil. This is so the tool can glide over your skin. It's best to do Gua Sha after cleansing your face.

Trigger Point Massage with White Flower Oil

My acupuncturist recommended that I try using White Flower Oil for my aches. When I did, I fell in love. Not only is White Flower Oil soothing, but it also comes with a very effective acupressure point treatment manual. I've read a few books on trigger and acupressure points, and I've found them not very user-friendly. Usually, these books share so many pressure points that you can't memorize them. This makes it harder to treat yourself regularly.

However, the pressure points shared in the White Flower manual are not only effective for every part of the body, but they're easy to commit to memory. Treating myself regularly with a pressure point massage is one of my favorite ways of releasing muscular stress from my body.

Unfortunately, sometimes you may come across a box of White Flower Oil without the pressure point manual, so here is a link where you can get a look at it[1].

White Flower Oil is not for everyone. It has a refreshing but strong scent, and some may find it irritating to their skin. Although I love using it, I know it was recommended to me because according to TCM, I had too much "heat" and the weather was hot. As the weather becomes cooler I may have to switch from White Flower Oil to Red Flower Oil.

If you find that White Flower Oil is not for you, you can massage the pressure points with other muscle relief products.

Besides White Flower Oil, I like using O2 Derm Relief and Philip Huang Organic Survival Balm for trigger point massages.

When massaging a trigger point, keep in mind the following:

- Gently rub the point in a circular motion or apply firm, steady pressure.

- Do not press so hard on a point that it hurts. Pain means stop.

- As you massage the area, look for a gentle, gradual release of tension.

---

1. https://drive.google.com/file/d/1j5kbFjEZCtdjP2SatoCtI3-BmOY-BRbW/view?usp=sharing

Epsom Salt Baths

Epsom salt baths are also very effective for releasing full body tension, and it is something I need to do more often!

You don't have to stick to buying regular vanilla Epsom salts. There are salts mixed with herbs and essential oils for extra relaxation. So test out different salts and have fun taking a bath.

Appreciate What Is Working in Your Life

Highly sensitive people are known for their tendency to worry. Being aware of so many details and taking in additional sensory information all the time can do that to a person.

When I notice that I am starting to feel overwhelmed with life, here are my two favorite lists to make:

- A list of what is currently working in my life.

- A list of good things that are appearing in my life that I didn't have to strive for.

These lists help me to switch my focus from what I need to fix to what I already have. Every time I take a moment to write about the good things, I feel the tension in my body melt away.

In general, try to make your self-care practices not only a moment of relaxation but a force for healing.

Self-care is a regular opportunity to release tension in your body and improve your health

Life Change #7: Practice Letting Go

As an HSP, not only do I clench my muscles in reaction to stress, but I also engage in emotional "clenching."

I tend to hold on to negative emotions, although they keep hurting me, just like it's hard for me to release and relax my achy muscles. I've had to incorporate practices for letting go emotionally into my life.

Practicing forgiveness towards others, especially myself, has been an effective tool for healing. At the start of my chronic pain issues, I spent so much energy being angry at myself, wondering how I could let this happen. But the truth is, I had no idea that things would turn out the way they did. And even if I did know, holding a grudge against myself wouldn't help me to get any better. Once I managed to forgive myself, I immediately felt a huge weight lift off of me, and I started to improve.

My favorite letting go practices are forgiveness, decluttering, saying goodbye, and journaling. This can also involve working with the messages within emotions[1], childhood wounds, and trauma. When it comes to the more emotional issues, there is nothing wrong with having a therapist help you work through them.

Forgiveness and letting go aren't about completely forgetting what happened. Often, it's impossible to do so. Instead, forgiveness is about releasing the grip of emotional pain. You go from a place of blame to a place of finding comfort, peace, and solutions.

So just as I shared some of my favorite self-care methods, here are some of my favorite letting-go practices and resources.

---

1. https://arcadiapage.com/2022-05-30-the-power-of-transforming-pain-into-art-for-infps/

Forgiveness Letters

This is the method I used to help myself to let go of all the self-directed guilt and anger I was carrying related to my health issues.

First, I wrote a sincere apology letter to myself. I apologized for failing to stay aware of my physical and emotional needs, expressed a ton of regret, and wrote about how I will do better in the future.

Then I imagined that I was receiving this apology letter from someone else. After reading it over, I wrote back, expressing how I felt about the situation, my appreciation of the apology, and my hopes for things to go better in the future.

Doing this helped me to be honest about my mistakes and to approach them with compassion. We all mess up sometimes, and that's okay. What matters is how we move forward from that.

Sometimes one letter of apology isn't enough. In my mind, I imagined apologizing to myself multiple times, and I always accepted and responded to each one with kindness.

I loved doing this so much because, little by little, I noticed that the harsh critical voice in my head had lost its grip over me, and I had more space to be more understanding and reasonable with myself.

Decluttering

Something about letting go of unnecessary items is refreshing. After I declutter, I feel like a breath of fresh air just came into my life.

Decluttering can be a huge project, and sometimes it needs to be. It's possible to have accumulated so much stuff that time needs to be dedicated to cleaning it all out.

However, sometimes circumstances don't allow for making decluttering this major event. Back when my chronic pain was worse, I was getting depressed because there was so much stuff in my surroundings that I didn't need, but I didn't have the energy to take care of it.

At that time, my husband said something that forever changed my view of decluttering. He said, "You don't have to take on the whole house. Just focus on your room." By my room, he meant my office, but by extension, he was alluding to taking care of my personal spaces first.

Of course, when decluttering, you should never take on spaces that exclusively belong to another person or throw out items that belong to someone else in your household. They need to do that for themselves. However, in a house, there are communal spaces, such as the living room and kitchen, and then there are spaces just for you. So focus on your personal areas before taking on shared space.

By shifting my focus from the entire house to my personal areas, decluttering went from a household chore to an act of self-care. For a week, I made a goal to spend 15 to 20 minutes a day decluttering my office. By the end of the week, I had fully decluttered my office, leaving myself surprised and impressed.

Every time we buy something, we purchase it with a set of expectations. We think about what we want it to accomplish, be it boosting our creativity, helping us make a meal, or simply making us look more beautiful. So when decluttering my office, I picked up every item and asked myself:

"Is this object working for me? Is it bringing into my life what I expected it to? Does it create positive feelings and peace, or does it create negative feelings?"

I admit that I am a Marie Kondo fan, but I find asking a few additional questions helpful in figuring out if something "sparks joy" for me.

I was amazed at how many objects I had around that had done nothing for me. Dried out ink pens. Unreliable ink pens. Notebooks that I didn't care for. Disappointing hair products. Outdated gadgets. These things did not bring into my life what I needed and expected.

Since I also tend to collect items related to hobbies and projects I'm working on, I also asked this additional question:

"Is this item related to a current task or project?"

By the way, this is also a great question to ask when cleaning up computer files.

If yes, then I'll keep it. If not, I'll run it through the previous questions to figure out what kind of feelings it creates for me. Sometimes extra supplies related to projects I wish to do one day create a lot of emotional stress. When a hobby that is supposed to be fun feels like a burden, it's time to reevaluate your approach.

If you're a person with a ton of hobbies and interests and need some advice on managing it all, you'll appreciate my other book, **I Want to Do All the Things: Finding Balance as a Polymath, Multipotentialite & Renaissance Soul.**

Saying Goodbye

Sometimes it's hard to let things go, be it physical items or memories. But when we think about the good things they've done for us or the lessons learned, letting go isn't as hard. It's coming from a place of appreciation instead of the fear of suddenly being without.

Thank you for all you've taught, shown, and accomplished. Please be well as we go our separate ways.

What I love the most about saying goodbye is it's an acknowledgment of things becoming a part of the past. Once that's recognized, it's time to release what used to be and move on to what's next.

Journaling

I don't habitually journal every day. Instead, I use my journal when I need it. If I'm feeling overwhelmed or confused, I do a journal entry. My main method of journaling is brain dumping. Letting out all the swirling thoughts gives my brain the space it needs to function. If your mind is going in circles from trying to hold on to all of your thoughts, you need to do a brain dump.

My second favorite way to journal is writing about how I feel. I don't overthink it. I start by writing, "Today I feel...," and then I keep going with whatever comes to mind.

I usually describe my feelings first and then dig into what's going on in my life and why I feel the way I do. If I'm struggling with negative emotions, I also think about what can be done to address them.

Another journaling prompt I like is the question, "What's working in my life right now?"

I use this prompt every time things feel out of control. When I take a moment to think about what's working instead of my problems, I realize everything isn't completely horrible and there is some hope for me after all.

Listening to the Messages Within Emotions

Knowing your emotions is essential for highly sensitive people. Learning to recognize them and what they are saying is how we begin to draw the line between the feelings that belong to us and others.

Doing this doesn't have to be complicated. Simply having a list of feeling words and seeing which of those apply to you every day is enough to start getting in touch with what you're feeling.

When facing the numbness of depression, I clearly remember how putting my emotions into specific words brought me to a point where I could see what I was honestly feeling. I thought I felt numb, but actually, I was disappointed, frustrated, and angry. Those feelings pointed to the things I didn't like, boundaries and limits that I needed to acknowledge, and actions I needed to take.

My favorite resource for dealing with emotions as a highly sensitive person is Eggshell Therapy[2], a website by Imi Lo. I recommend checking out her podcast, her books, and the many exercises she shares for riding the waves of your emotions as a highly sensitive person.

Childhood Wounds

Everyone has them. You can have great parents and a childhood full of love and still have childhood wounds. This is because our parents are human. They make mistakes, and as children, our interpretations of those mistakes can haunt us for our entire lives. While growing up, we also face social and generational pressures. So dealing with childhood wounds is about letting go of the unhelpful coping patterns and beliefs you held on to as a child.

This is especially important for HSPs because often the emotional issues surrounding our childhood wounds are tied up with how we view being sensitive. And if you don't face your childhood hurts, you'll be prone to using negative and immature coping methods for the rest of your life.

Being aware of and working with my childhood wounds has been essential to my mental health overall. Doing this has allowed me to take ownership of my personal power and ability to make choices. You

2. https://eggshelltherapy.com/

realize that you are not a child anymore, and you don't have to cope with your problems like you did when you were less capable. It's not about fixating on who to blame. It's about finally seeing life through the eyes of a capable adult and becoming aware of how your childhood understanding of things could use some updating.

One of my favorite books about handling childhood wounds is **How to Overcome Your Childhood** by The School of Life. There are things I disagree with in many of the books I read, and this book is no exception. But I have to say that this book handled a subject that can get complicated in the most straightforward way, and it gave me a gentle awareness of the childhood beliefs that have been standing in my way.

I also like how this book highlights the humanness of parents. As little kids, we fall into thinking that our parents are all powerful and even perfect. Being aware of the oh-so-human mistakes of my parents has made me connect with them from a place of understanding, even if some of our interactions impacted me negatively. And on another level, it helps parents to see that making mistakes in child rearing is inevitable, but that's okay because they can still give their children the emotional tools they need to separate themselves from the mistakes of their caregivers.

Another good resources for working with childhood wounds is the Enneagram personality type system. In fact, it was through my work with my childhood wounds that I found my correct Enneagram type (I'm an SX/SP 3w4, by the way).

What I like about the Enneagram is that it gives practical ways of dealing with and overcoming childhood wounds. For example, my biggest childhood wound centers around over-achievement. This corresponds with the Type 3 on the Enneagram. This need for admiration and achievement is woven throughout my entire life. According to the Enneagram, slowing down, getting in touch with my definition of success, and remembering my existence alone makes me worthy of love is the cure.

The way the Enneagram handles healing from your past makes it a great for psychological growth. The Enneagram involves handling the emotional issues surrounding anger, shame, and fear, and how they appear in your life. I've never gone to an Enneagram-focused therapist, but they are out there. A therapist trained in the Enneagram can help you lean into the strengths of your type while overcoming your past.

My favorite book on the Enneagram is **Enneagram Empowerment: Discover Your Personality Type and Unlock Your Potential** by Laura Miltenberger. This book lead me to finally typing myself correctly[3]. By the way, figuring out your Enneagram type involves more than just taking the test. Sometimes your test results may only point to one of your wings or the characteristics of another type that is close to yours. The most important thing to look at is the motivations and desires. Your Enneagram type is the one with the desires and motivations that have impacted you the most.

There is no need to rush to figure out your correct type. For a long time, I thought I was a Type 4, and this knowledge encouraged me to deal with my other childhood wound of feeling misunderstood and inherently lacking. It took moving beyond that for me to finally see the main issue that I needed to face. So when it comes to the Enneagram, relax into it and learn to deal with whatever you discover within yourself.

Another book on the Enneagram that I like is **The Honest Enneagram** by Sarajane Case. I like her practical and to-the-point advice for each of the types.

If you want to dive into inner child work, I recommend checking out **The Undervalued Self** by Dr. Elaine Aron. Doing all of this can get intense,

---

3. https://arcadiapage.com/2022-09-30-what-it-s-like-being-an-infp-enneagram-type-3/

so if you feel unsafe or need more support, reach out to a therapist. And once again, don't rush it. Take your time and let the journey unfold.

Let go from a place of
appreciation instead of
the fear of suddenly
being without

HSP Care Made Easy

I'm probably only speaking for myself here, but whenever I see an online article entitled "100 Things Highly Sensitive People Can Do for Self-Care," I feel like my head is going to explode. Having so many options is nice, but I think the issue is that I feel the pressure of thinking that I need to do all 100 things.

Taking care of yourself as a highly sensitive person can be a struggle sometimes. It takes effort to figure out what self-care practices to keep in your life and what to let go of. So, my goal here is to reduce the overwhelm and to make things easier for you.

I know I've already shared many ways to take care of yourself in this book, but you don't have to do all of them. Instead, pick one thing for each of these areas:

Pick one thing to take care of your **body**. What is one thing you can do to release stress from your body?

Pick one thing to take care of your **mind**. What is one thought that can help you to improve your mindset in a meaningful way?

Pick one thing to take care of your **emotions**. What is one practice you can add to your life for your emotional health?

Do whatever activities you've come across so far that attract you the most. Anything you're feeling pulled towards is worthy of going on the list. If you try something for a while but see that it's not for you, feel free to switch it out with something else.

You are Productive

The hectic pace of modern life can give us a twisted view of what it means to be productive. I dive into this concept a bit more in my other book **Thoughtful Planning: How to Use Questions for Self-reflection to Design Your Day**, but here are the basics.

As highly sensitive people, we can sometimes feel like we're falling behind because we need to approach life at a slower pace. I found this to be especially painful because as a chronic over-achiever, I believed that if I couldn't hustle like everyone else, I wouldn't be able to earn the love that I needed to exist in this world. As a result, I became a workaholic and a caffeine addict, and the stress of trying to carry it all almost destroyed me.

I'm letting you know that your natural pace is perfectly fine. You don't need to kill yourself hustling like everyone else, and you don't need to prove anything to anyone. It's refreshing and creative to approach things in a way that comes naturally to you.

You are being productive when:

- You take care of yourself. Napping is productivity. So is taking the time to create a healthy meal.

- You break your focus and "hustle" to show love and care to another part of your life.

- You decide to wait patiently before making a decision because you need time and space to consider more information.

- You take time to daydream about the kind of future you want to have.

- You take a walk outside and give your mind space to wander and assimilate ideas.

Living with love and care is the best way to produce a life that is authentic to your needs. This is what productivity should be about.

Living with love and care is the best way to produce a life that is authentic to your needs.

Some Parting Thoughts

So these are all the things I wish I knew I needed in my life as a highly sensitive person. I'm sure that as I continue on my journey, I'll discover more things that will help me to create a life that honors my sensitivity, and I'm sure you will too.

At the very least, find something you can incorporate into your life regularly, daily if possible, to show that you respect your sensitive nature. Personally, I've benefited a lot from trying to make time every day for reflection or a short nap.

If you're not sure where to start, revisit the chapter *HSP Care Made Easy.*

What three activities did you pick to nourish your mind, body, and emotions?

Out of those three things, can any of those be done within 10 minutes or less? If there's nothing, can you adjust anything to fit that time frame?

Once you figure out a practice you can do within that time, ask yourself, "Can I do this every day?"

If not, make some changes so you can do one small act of honoring your sensitivity every day. It's the small things we do that make the most impact. Consistency is more important than intensity. Besides, your sensitivity is a gift that doesn't have on and off days. It's there all the time. So it's best to learn how to accommodate it every day.

For more articles about life as a sensitive, creative, intuitive person, subscribe to my blog[1]. Not only do I share more lessons learned related

---

1. https://tinyletter.com/arcadiapage

to being highly sensitive and a curious and creative individual, but since I'm an INFP on the MBTI, also I write articles for INFPs.

Thank you for reading!

Thank you!

Don't miss out!

Visit the website below and you can sign up to receive emails whenever Arcadia Page publishes a new book. There's no charge and no obligation.

https://books2read.com/r/B-A-XZED-XVECC

BOOKS 2 READ

Connecting independent readers to independent writers.

Also by Arcadia Page

Idealist Dreams: How I Learned to Plan as an INFP
I Want to Do All the Things: Finding Balance as a Polymath,
Multipotentialite & Renaissance Soul
I Can't Help Being an INFP Writer
The Little Book of Tiny Tasks: Make Your Life More Calm While
Getting Things Done 5 Minutes at a Time
Thoughtful Planning: How to Use Questions for Self-reflection to
Design Your Day
Love Your Sensitivity: 7 Essential Life Changes to Make after Learning
You're a Highly Sensitive Person

Watch for more at www.arcadiapage.com.

About the Author

Arcadia Page is a writer and artist from central Florida. When she's not writing, she enjoys drawing, reading, and crafting. She shares her life with her husband, who also enjoys writing stories.

Read more at www.arcadiapage.com.